MOST DANGEROUS DESERTS IN THE WORLD

DESERTS OF THE WORLD FOR KIDS CHILDREN'S EXPLORE THE WORLD BOOKS

Speedy Publishing LLC

40 E. Main St. #1156

Newark, DE 19711

www.speedypublishing.com

Copyright 2017

In this book, we're going to talk all about the most dangerous deserts in the world. So, let's get right to it!

About one fifth of the landmass worldwide is composed of dry, barren deserts, which get very little precipitation, about 10 inches or less annually. Deserts are some of the most dangerous places to be on Earth. Deserts are characterized by their lack of water and this is certainly one of the aspects that make them dangerous to people.

Extreme temperatures, both hot and cold, are another reason that deserts are dangerous. Sudden dust storms in hot deserts and severe freezing winds in polar deserts are also a threat.

A nimals that live in deserts, such as scorpions and snakes that can kill with their deadly venoms, large mammal carnivorous predators such as polar bears in the Arctic regions, and leopards in Africa, pose deadly risks for those traveling through the desert as well.

THE SAHARA DESERT–AFRICA

The Sahara Desert is the largest expanse of dry, hot land on Earth. It encompasses about 9.4 million square kilometers, which is more landmass than the United States and is the largest desert that isn't a polar desert. The word Sahara means "The Great Desert" in the Arabic language and it is certainly true to that name since it covers most of North Africa and extends through more than ten different countries.

There are frequent sand storms as well as dust devils, which are funnel-shaped dust clouds kicked up by high winds. In fact, the winds from the northeast can reach the speeds of hurricanes. One of the deadly animals that lives in the Sahara is the venomous deathstalker scorpion. It can grow to a length of 4 inches and carries two deadly toxins.

THE ANTARCTIC DESERT–ANTARCTICA

We generally think of deserts as regions with very high temperatures but deserts can be cold as well. The entire continent of Antarctica is the largest polar desert on the face of planet Earth and it's covered in sheets of ice. The harsh climate of freezing temperatures and wind makes it impossible for people to live there in permanent settlements. Some areas of the Antarctic desert have had no rain for over 2 million years!

THE ARABIAN DESERT– ARABIAN PENINSULA

The Arabian Desert spans the Arabian peninsula from the country of Yemen to the country of Iraq. This desert has very dangerous areas of quicksand, which can entrap you and pull you underground. The temperatures vary from searing, unbearable dry heat of 129 degrees Fahrenheit to below freezing within a 24-hour span of time.

THE ATACAMA DESERT-CHILE

Located in the country of Chile, the Atacama Desert has regions that haven't had any rain for over 400 years! Because of the harsh conditions, few animals or plants can survive there, but in rare cases after there has been some rainfall there are huge fields of flowers.

THE ARCTIC DESERT— THE ARCTIC CIRCLE

The Arctic is a cold, polar desert that receives about the same amount of precipitation yearly as the Sahara Desert. The freezing temperatures make this region inhospitable for most people, but different groups of Inuit people have lived there for thousands of years.

THE GOBI DESERT– CHINA AND MONGOLIA

The Gobi Desert, which covers a huge expanse of 800,000 square miles, is unusual because it has dry and wet seasons including a dangerous monsoon season.

THE SYRIAN DESERT– THE MIDDLE EAST

The Syrian Desert covers much of the country of Iraq as well as Syria, Saudi Arabia, and Jordan. This arid wasteland was impossible for humans to cross until recent decades although in ancient times parts of it were accessible to people.

In 2009, an ancient circle of stones created by people was discovered and dubbed "Syria's Stonehenge." The largest field of volcanic activity, called the Es Safa volcanic field, is located there. In addition to the dangerous natural occurrences in the Syrian Desert, it has been a hotbed of world political conflict for many decades.

THE KALAHARI DESERT—AFRICA

The word "Kalahari" means "immense thirst." This desert is a huge expanse of hot red sand in Africa that covers about 360,000 square miles. In addition to the dangerous heat and lack of water, this desert is home to many big cats like lions and cheetahs. The Kalahari Desert covers large areas of the country of South Africa as well as the countries of Botswana and Namibia.

THE NAMIB DESERT–AFRICA

Scientists believe that the Namib Desert in Africa may be the oldest desert worldwide. It has been an arid region for more than 50 million years. The animals that have survived here have amazing adaptations like the Tenebrionid beetle. It's able to roll a tiny fog droplet down its back and channel it into its mouth so it can drink.

THE MOJAVE DESERT- UNITED STATES

The driest desert on the North American continent, the Mojave desert is home to the aptly named Death Valley. One of the highest temperatures ever recorded happened there in 1913, when it was 134 degrees Fahrenheit.

In addition to the searing temperatures the desert is home to dangerous cougars and rattlesnakes. Gila monsters, which are venomous lizards, lurk between the rocks.

THE TAKLAMAKAN DESERT–CHINA

The extremes of temperature in the Taklamakan desert in China make it one of the deadliest places on Earth. It gets less than 1 centimeter of rainfall every year and at night the cold temperatures are severe.

The record low temperature there was -25 degrees Fahrenheit. Some of the physical features of the Taklamakan desert are called the "Place of Ruins" as well as the "Sea of Death."

THE PATAGONIAN DESERT-ARGENTINA

Covering most of Argentina, the cold Patagonian Desert extends for over 260,000 square miles. Like many other deserts, it was formed by a "rain shadow." A rain shadow is when a very high mountain range creates a barrier that stops rain from penetrating into a location.

In this case, the enormous mountain range of the Andes prevents water from getting into the Patagonian Desert.
Galina Safronova

THE GREAT VICTORIAN DESERT–AUSTRALIA

Covering 250,000 square miles, the Great Victorian desert in Australia has red sand dunes and salt lakes. It's a harsh environment with around 6.4 inches of annual rainfall.

Despite this, there are many animals that manage to thrive there including camels that weren't native to the region but were brought there in the 19th century from Arabia and India to help with construction work in the outback.

There are now over 750,000 wild camels there and they are causing destruction for farmers and ranchers and destroying habitats for other native animals by drinking the scarce water that's available.

THE GREAT BASIN DESERT–UNITED STATES

Most of the precipitation in the Great Basin desert falls as snow. This desert covers a large portion of Nevada, a section of Utah, and regions of surrounding states as well. The strong winds called the Santa Ana winds are one of the regions weather hazards. After forming in the desert, the winds frequently blow into the southern regions of California.

THE CHIHUAHUAN DESERT-UNITED STATES AND MEXICO

The Chihuahuan desert covers sections of Mexico and the United States, namely the state of Texas and the states of New Mexico as well as Arizona. There is little rainfall there, less than 9 inches annually. It's the largest desert in America covering 175,000 square miles.

The temperatures in the Chihuahuan desert vary from winter temperatures below zero degrees Fahrenheit to the searing heat of summer months when the temperature sometimes soars to 122 degrees Fahrenheit. The desert is home to deadly venomous animals, such as rattlesnakes and Gila monsters.

THE KARAKUM DESERT–CENTRAL ASIA

There is a crater in the Karakum Desert of Central Asia that has been burning natural gas for about 46 years. The local people called this fiery cauldron the "Gates of Hell." It began when geologists were concerned about a cave that was filled with deadly methane gas. They thought it would poison the area so they set the gas on fire.

SUMMARY

Deserts are arid regions where there is less than 10 inches of precipitation annually. Deserts can be scorching hot or freezing cold and sometimes they're both within the same 24-hour time period. The lack of available water, desert wind and dust storms, unbearable temperatures, and dangerous venomous animals make most of the world's deserts hazardous for people.

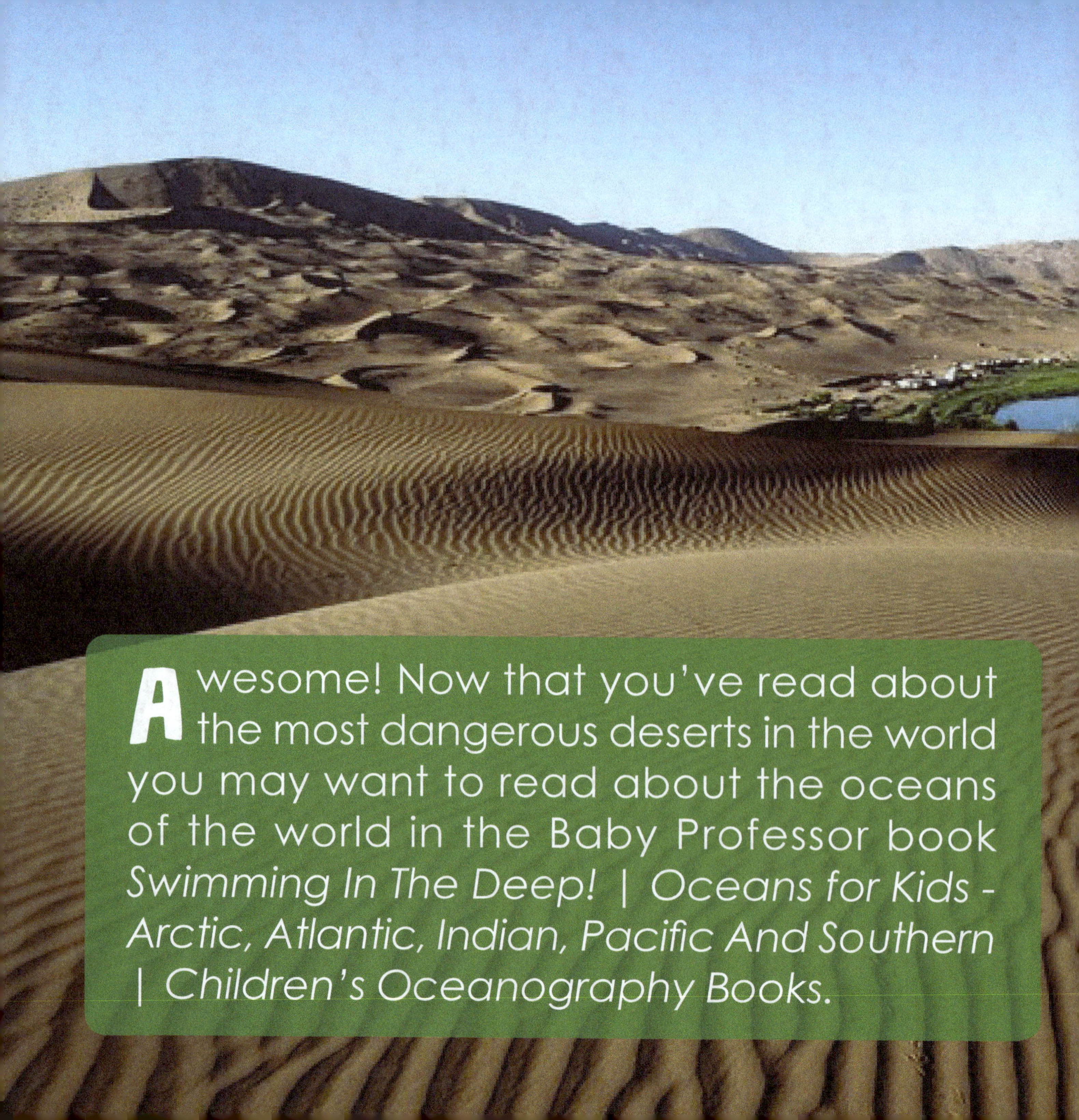

Awesome! Now that you've read about the most dangerous deserts in the world you may want to read about the oceans of the world in the Baby Professor book Swimming In The Deep! | Oceans for Kids - Arctic, Atlantic, Indian, Pacific And Southern | Children's Oceanography Books.

Visit

BABY PROFESSOR
EDUCATION KIDS

www.BabyProfessorBooks.com
to download Free Baby Professor eBooks
and view our catalog of new and exciting
Children's Books